BABY MINE

from DUMBO

Words by NED WASHINGTON
Music by FRANK CHURCHILL

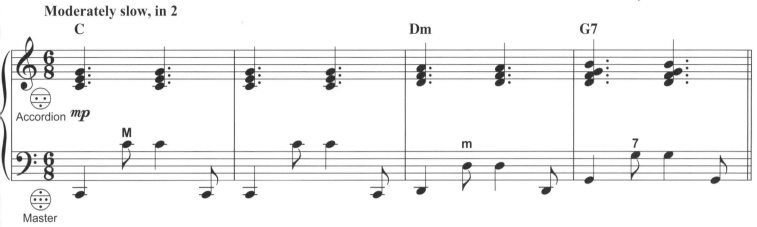

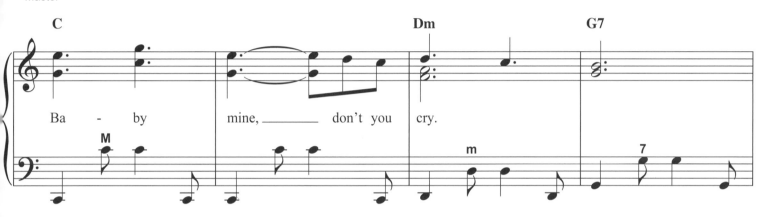

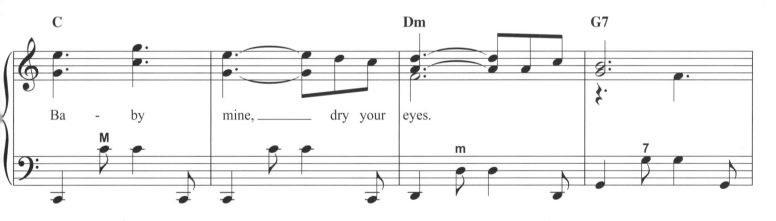

4

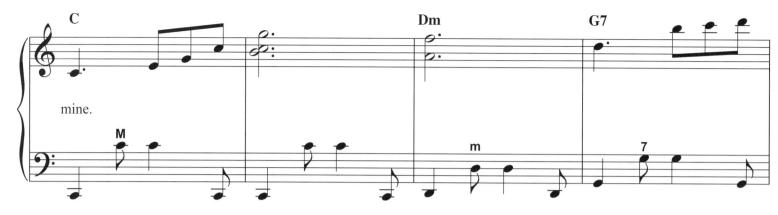

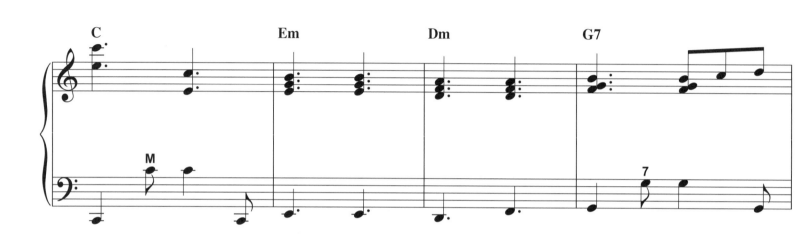

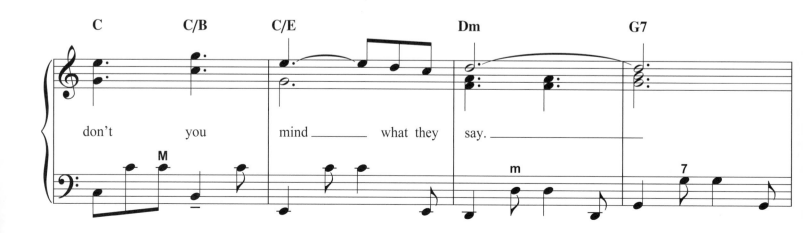

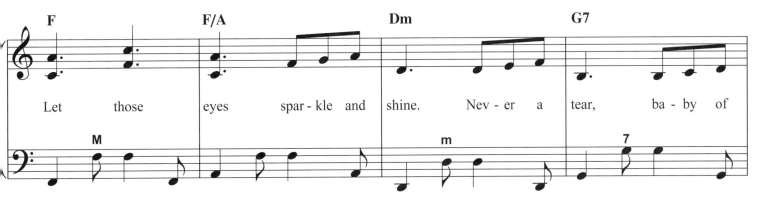

Let those eyes spar-kle and shine. Nev-er a tear, ba-by of

mine.

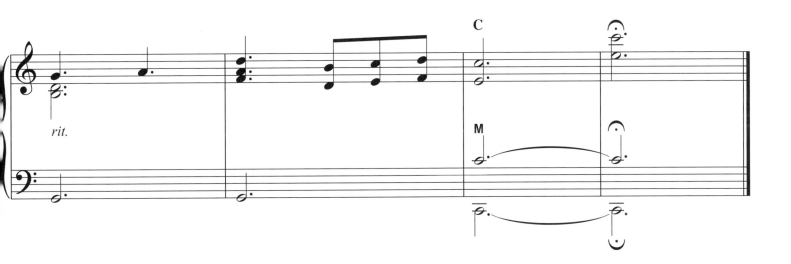

rit.

EVERMORE

from BEAUTY AND THE BEAST (2017)

Music by ALAN MENKEN
Lyrics by TIM RICE

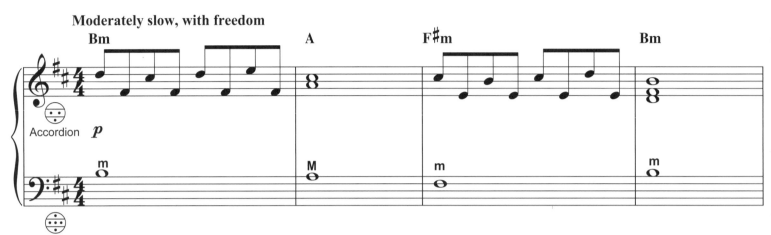

I was the one ___ who had it all; ___ I was the mas - ter ___ of my

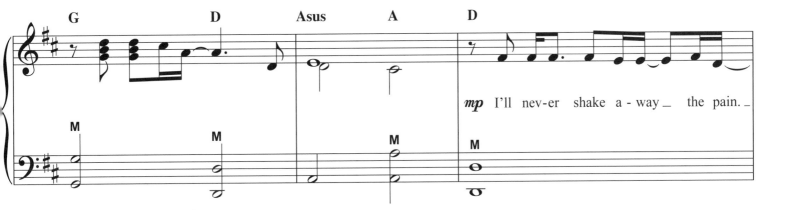

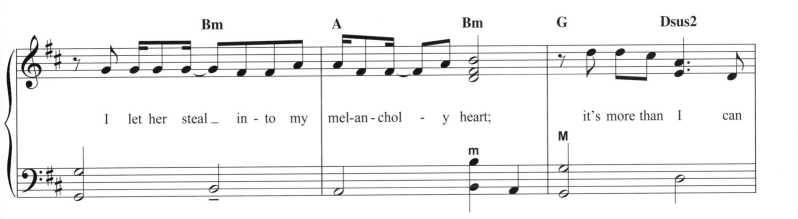

bear. Now I know she'll nev - er leave me, e-ven

as she runs a - way. She will still tor - ment _ me, calm me, hurt _ me, move _

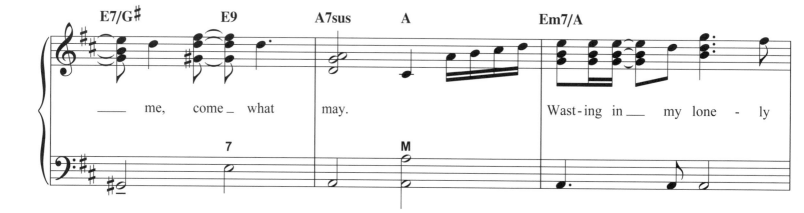

_ me, come _ what may. Wast - ing in _ my lone - ly

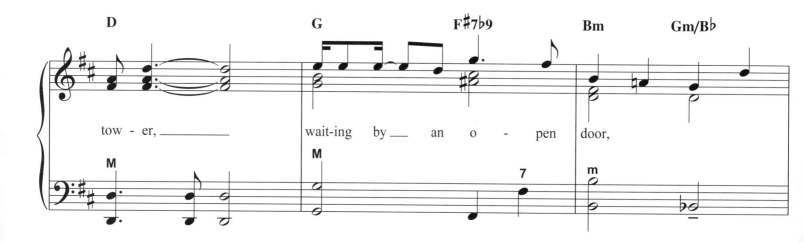

tow - er, _____ wait - ing by _ an o - pen door,

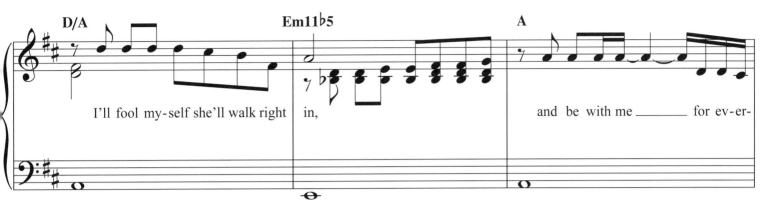

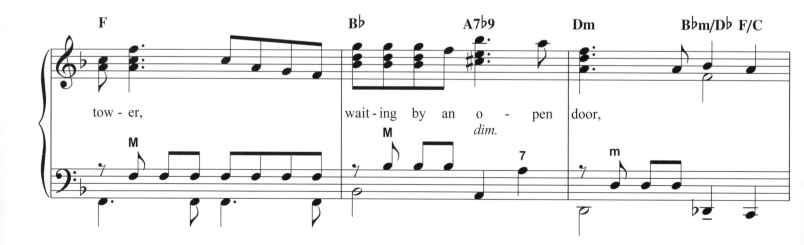

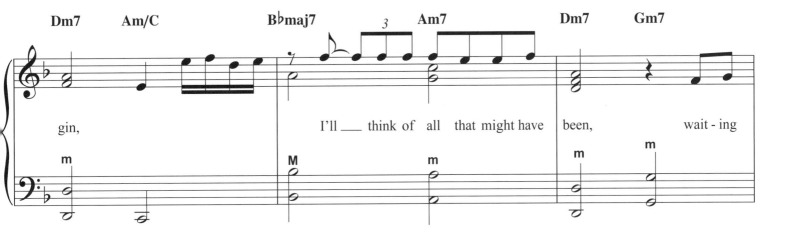

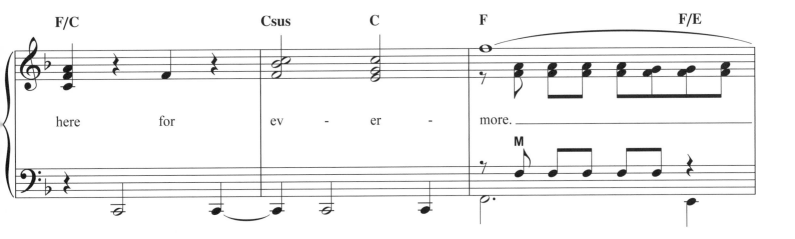

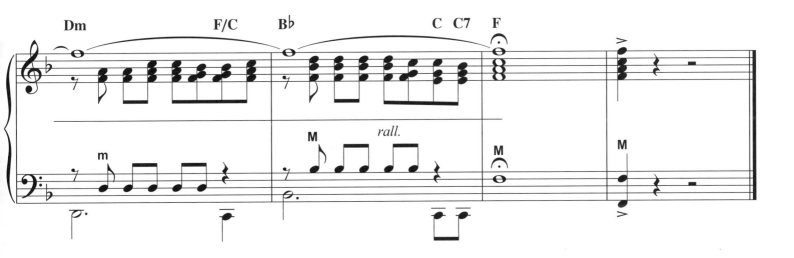

FOR THE FIRST TIME IN FOREVER

from FROZEN

Music and Lyrics by KRISTEN ANDERSON-LOPEZ
and ROBERT LOPEZ

With excitement

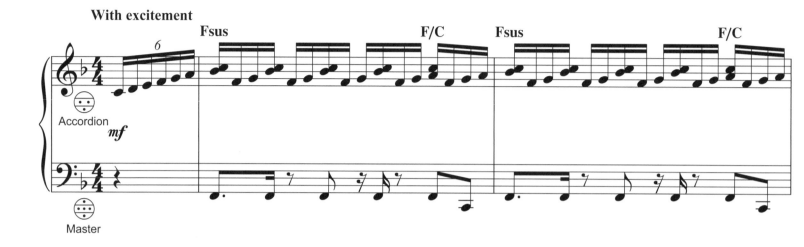

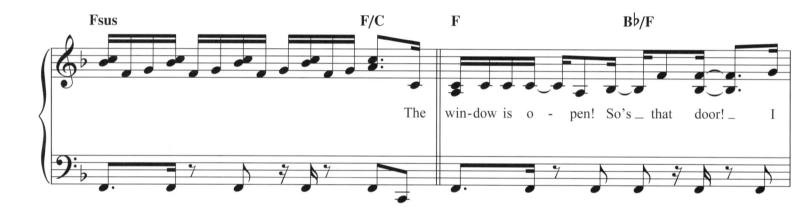

The win-dow is o - pen! So's _ that door! _ I

did-n't know they did that an - y - more. _ Who knew we owned _ eight thou - sand sal - ad

13

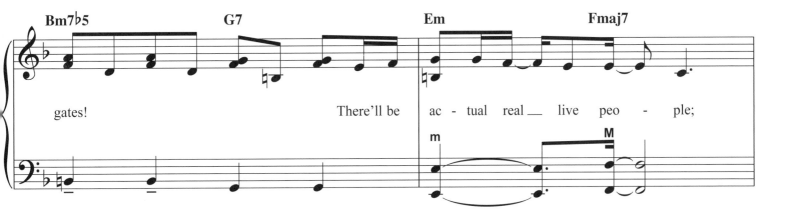

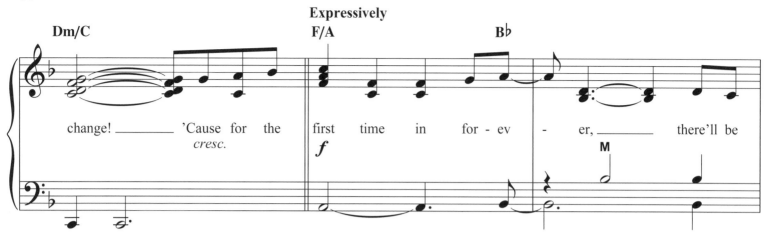

some-where in ___ that zone. 'Cause for the first time in for-ev-

- er, I won't be ___ a - lone.

Excited again

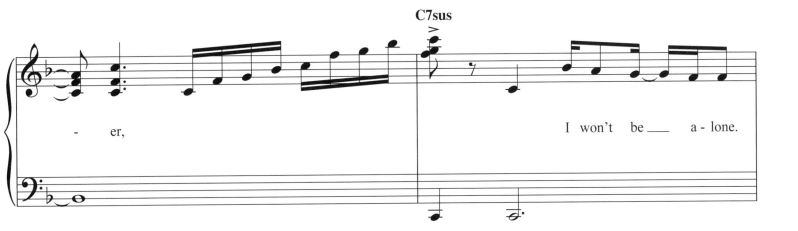

To - night, i-mag - ine me, gown ___ and all, ___

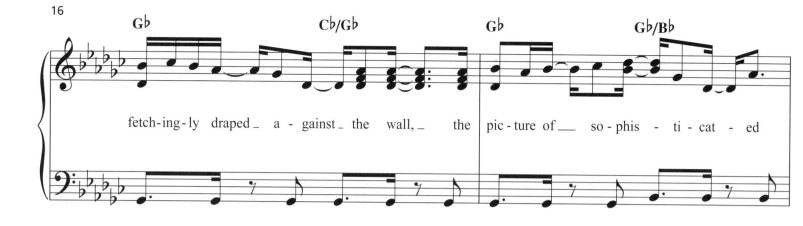

fetch-ing-ly draped _ a - gainst _ the wall, _ the pic-ture of _ so - phis - ti - cat - ed

grace. I sud-den-ly see _ him stand - ing there: _ a

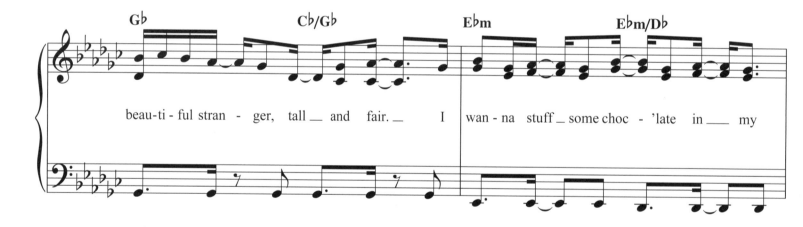

beau-ti - ful stran - ger, tall _ and fair. _ I wan - na stuff _ some choc - 'late in _ my

face! But then we laugh and talk _ all eve - ning, _ which is

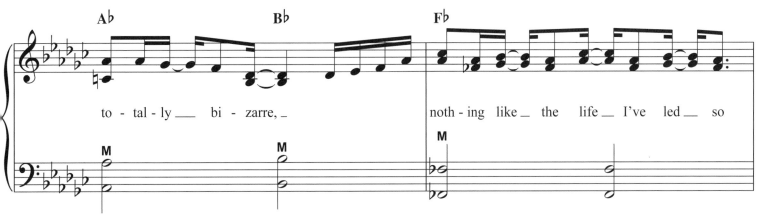

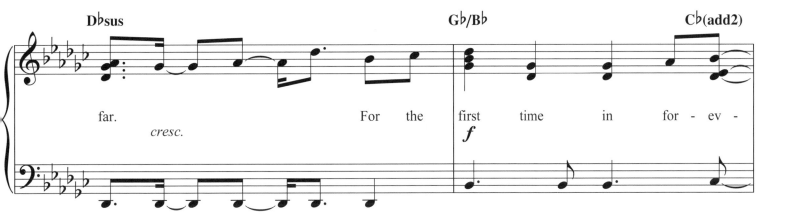

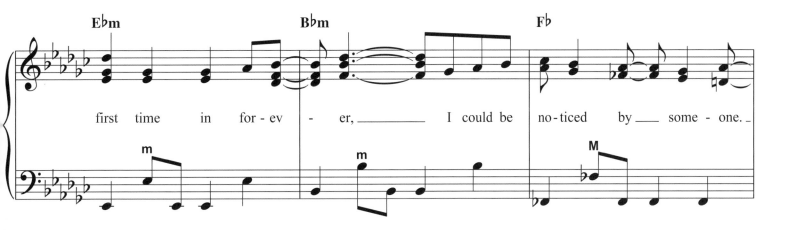

And I know it is to-tal-ly cra - zy ___ to

dream I'd find __ ro - mance, but for the first time in for - ev -

- er at least I've got __ a chance. __

HAKUNA MATATA
from THE LION KING

Music by ELTON JOHN
Lyrics by TIM RICE

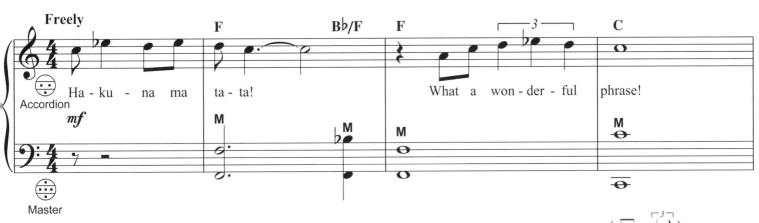

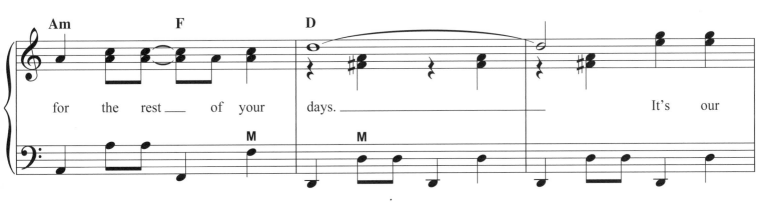

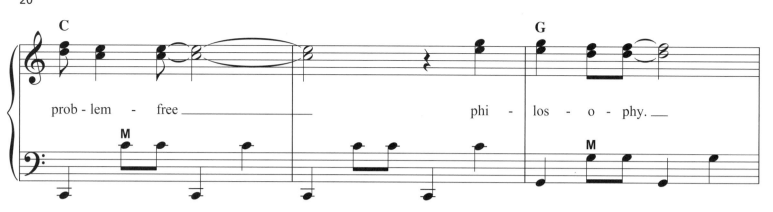

prob - lem - free _____ phi - los - o - phy. _____

Ha - ku - na ma - ta - ta. _____

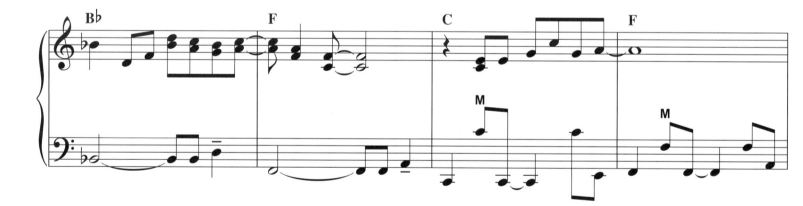

When

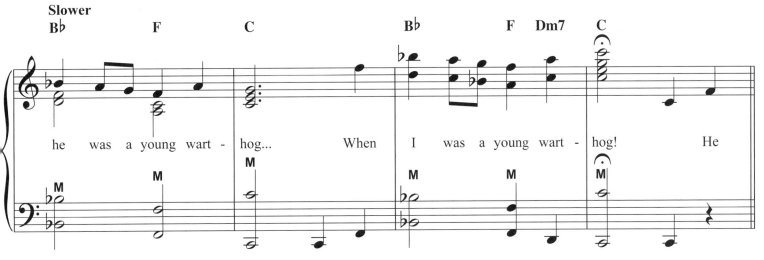

Slower

he was a young wart - hog... When I was a young wart - hog! He

In tempo, brightly

found his a - ro - ma lacked a cer - tain ap - peal. __ He could clear the Sa - van - nah af - ter

ev - 'ry meal. __ *I'm a sensitive soul,* *though I seem thick -*

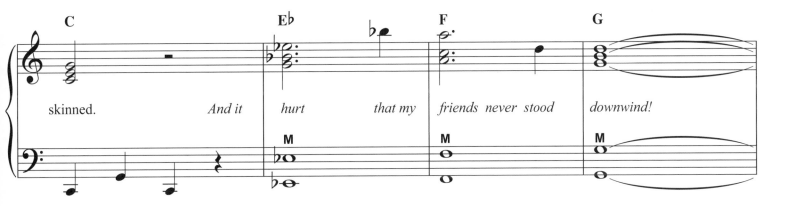

skinned. *And it hurt* *that my* *friends never stood* *downwind!*

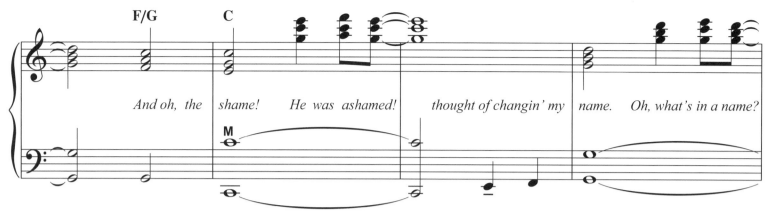

F/G C

And oh, the shame! He was ashamed! thought of changin' my name. Oh, what's in a name?

Bb   **In tempo** C

And I got downhearted.   How did ya feel?   Ev'ry time that I...   Ha - ku - na ma -

F   C

ta - ta!   What a won-der-ful   phrase.

F   D7   G   Am Bb dim

Ha - ku - na ma - ta - ta_____   ain't no pass - ing   craze!

23

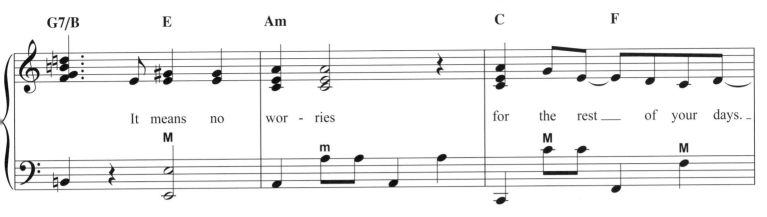

It means no wor - ries for the rest ___ of your days.___

It's our prob - lem - free ___ phi -

los - o - phy. ___ Ha - ku - na ma - ta - ta. ___

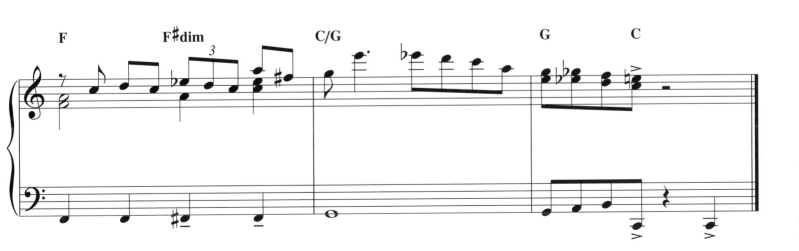

HE'S A PIRATE

from PIRATES OF THE CARIBBEAN: THE CURSE OF THE BLACK PEARL

Written by HANS ZIMMER,
KLAUS BADELT and GEOFF ZANELLI

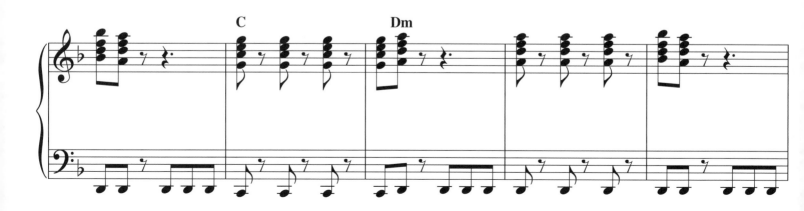

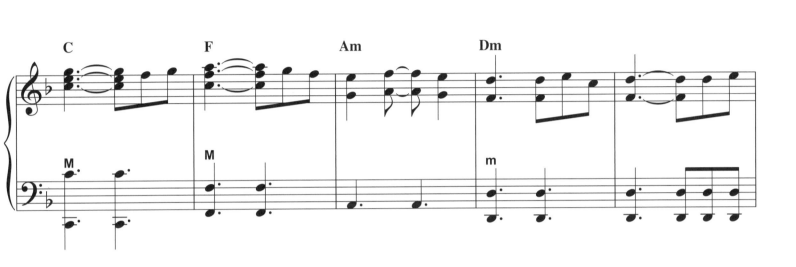

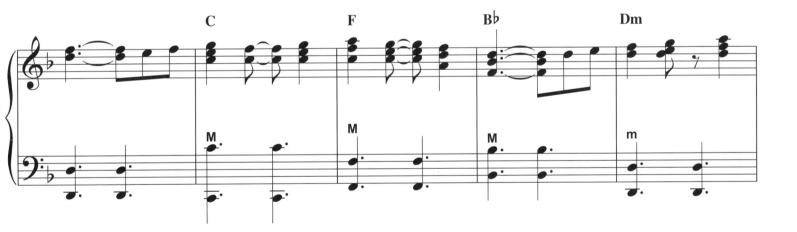

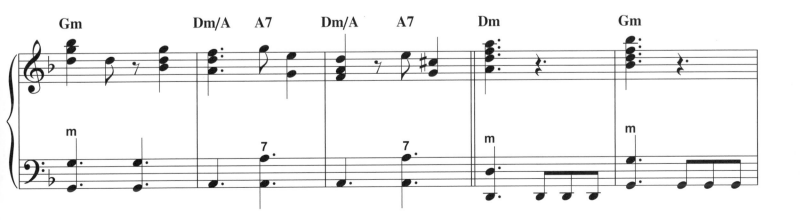

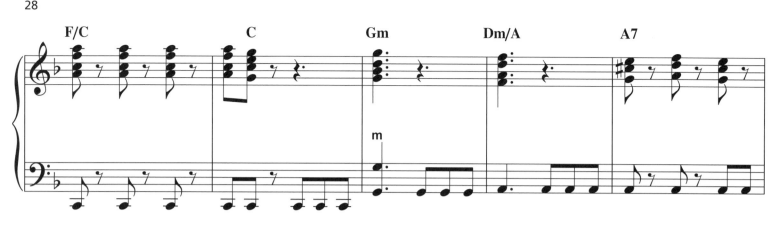

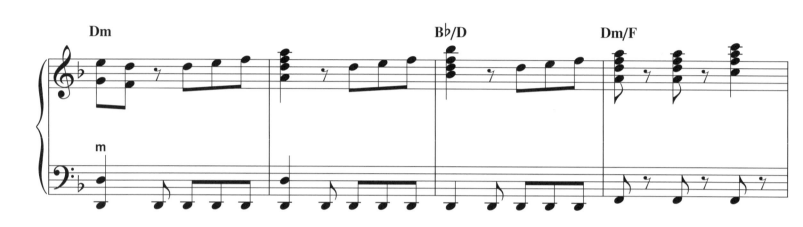

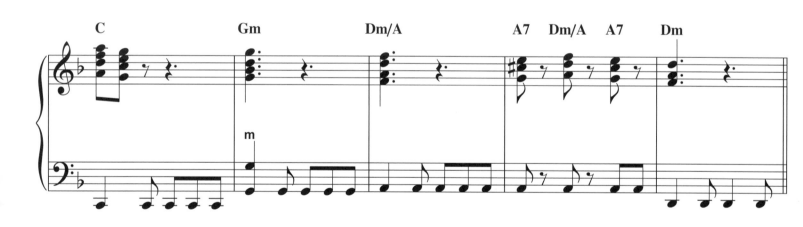

INTO THE UNKNOWN

from FROZEN 2

Music and Lyrics by KRISTEN ANDERSON-LOPEZ
and ROBERT LOPEZ

Mysteriously

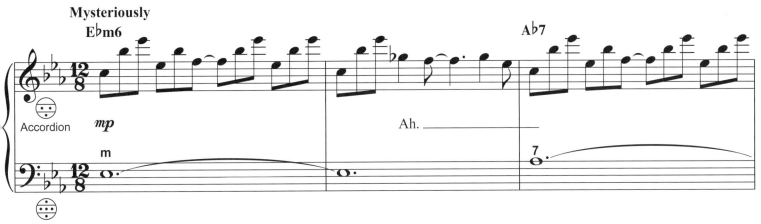

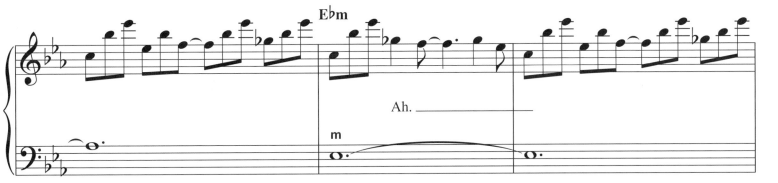

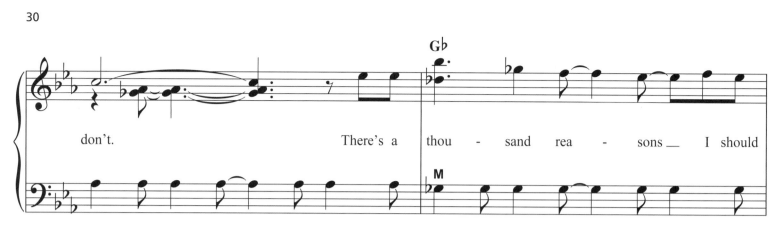

don't.   There's a   thou - sand rea - sons __ I should

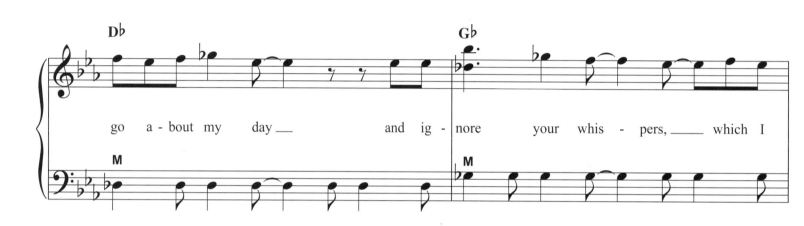

go a - bout my day __   and ig - nore   your whis - pers, __ which I

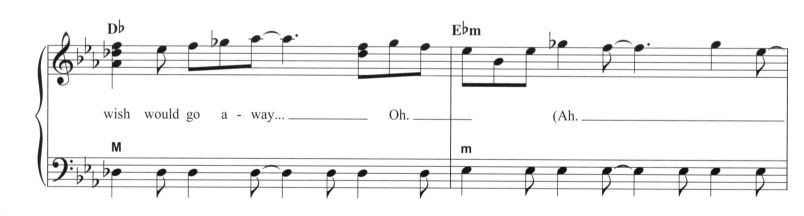

wish would go a - way... ____ Oh. __   (Ah. _____

____ Oh. ____   Ah.) _____ You're _ not a

With determination

voice, you're just a ring - ing in my ear, __ and __ if I

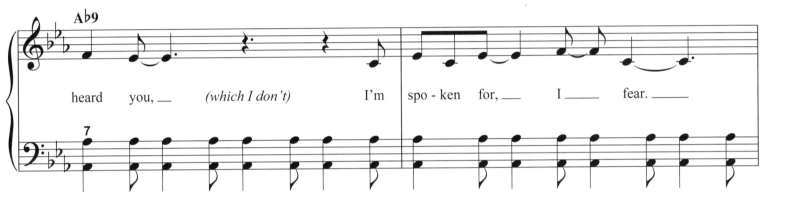

heard you, __ *(which I don't)* I'm spo - ken for, __ I __ fear. __

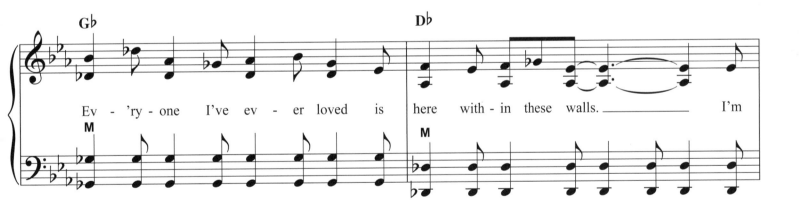

Ev - 'ry - one I've ev - er loved is here with - in these walls. _____ I'm

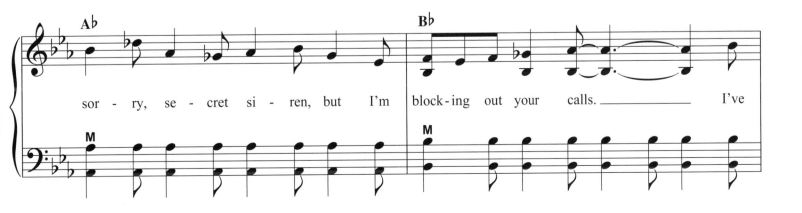

sor - ry, se - cret si - ren, but I'm block - ing out your calls. _____ I've

had my ad - ven - ture. I don't need some-thing new! __ I'm a-

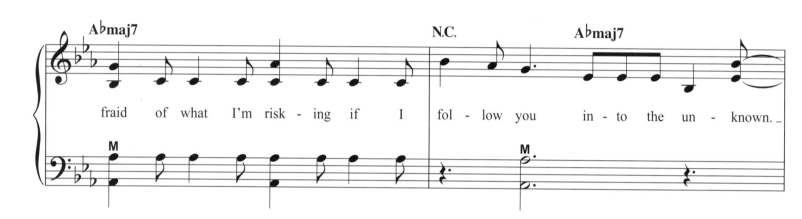

fraid of what I'm risk - ing if I fol - low you in - to the un - known. __

In - to the un - known... __

in - to the un - known! __

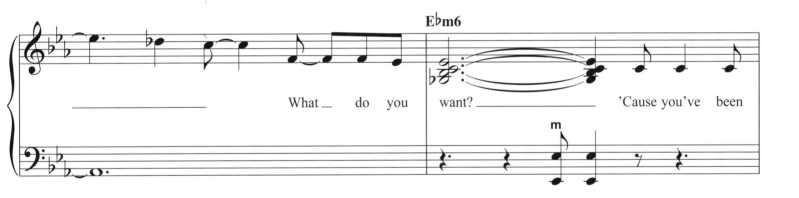

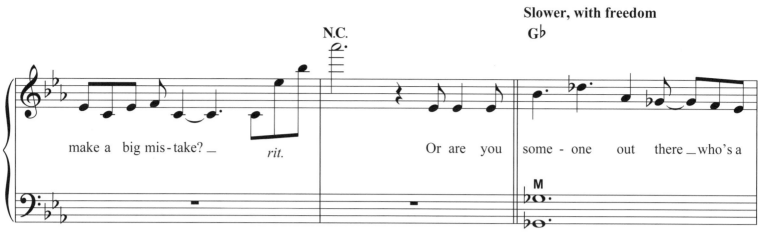

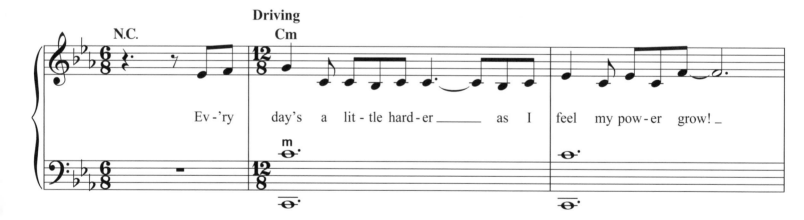

Into the un - known! _

Into the un - known! _

(Ah, _____ ah, _____

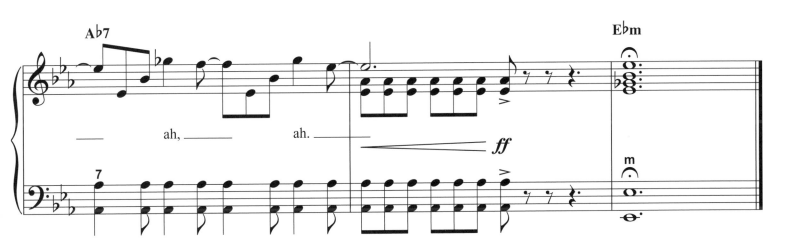

ah, _____ ah. _____

ff

REMEMBER ME
(Ernesto de la Cruz)
from COCO

Music and Lyrics by KRISTEN ANDERSON-LOPEZ
and ROBERT LOPEZ

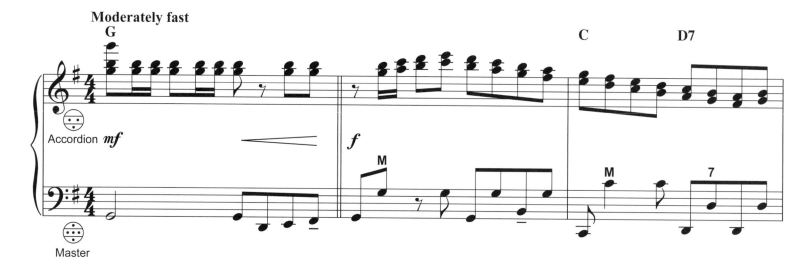

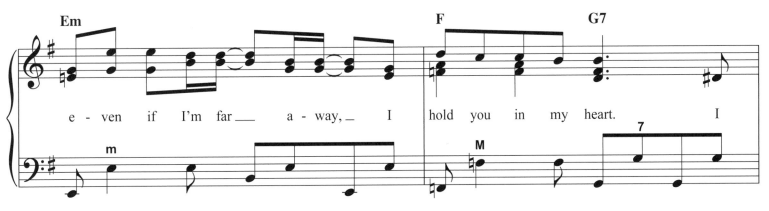

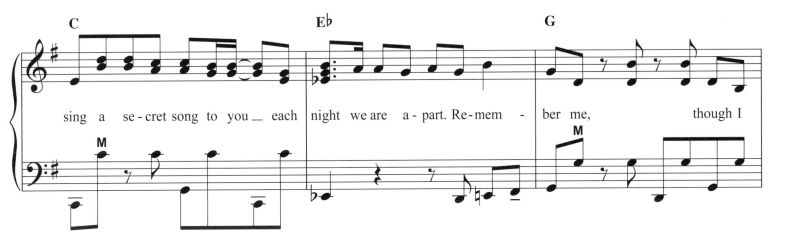

gain, re-mem - ber me. Re - mem - ber

me, though I have to say good-bye. _ Re-mem - ber me, don't

let it make you cry. For e - ven if I'm far a - way, _ I hold you in my heart. I

sing a se-cret song to you each night we are a - part. Re-mem - ber me, though I

have to trav-el far.___ Re-mem-ber me each time you

hear a sad gui-tar. Know that I'm with you the on-ly

way that I can be. Un-til you're in my arms a-gain, re-

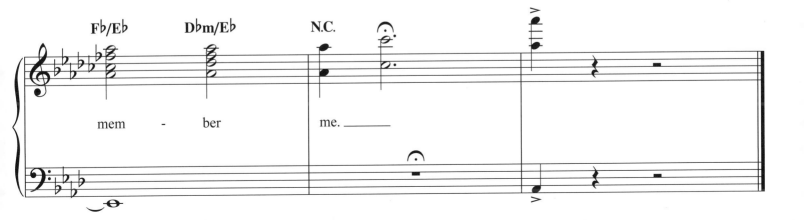

mem - ber me.___

SOME DAY MY PRINCE WILL COME

from SNOW WHITE AND THE SEVEN DWARFS

Words by LARRY MOREY
Music by FRANK CHURCHILL

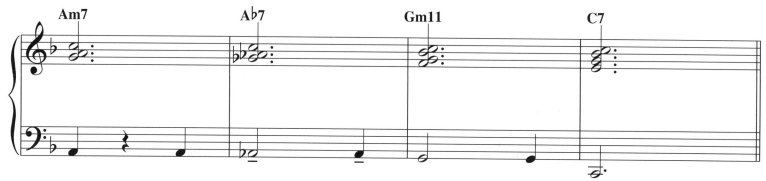

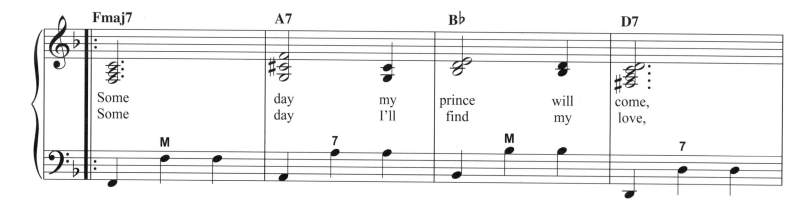

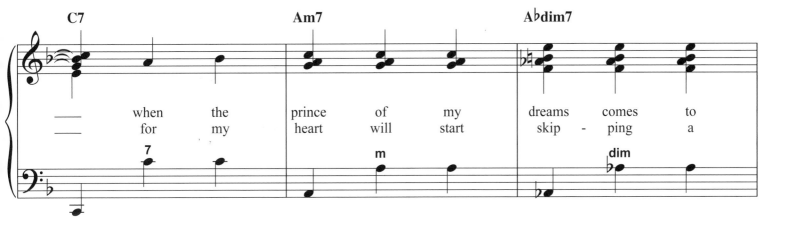

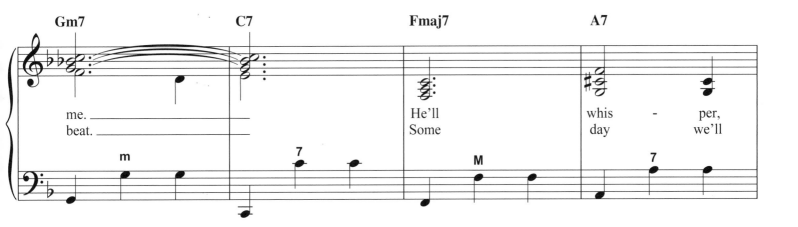

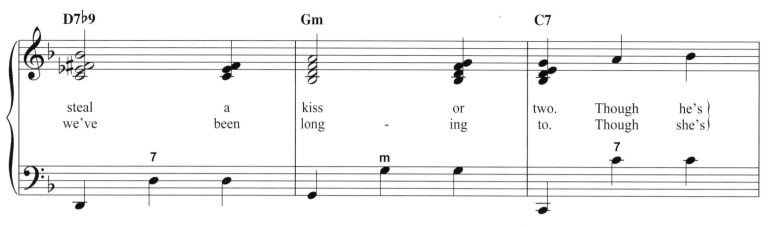

steal   a   kiss   or   two.   Though   he's
we've   been   long -   ing   to.   Though   she's

far   a -   way   I'll   find   my   love some   day,   some

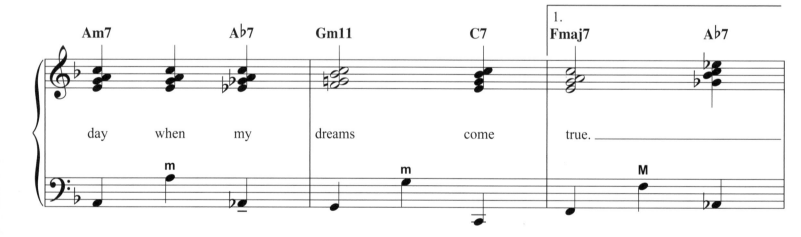

day   when   my   dreams   come   true.

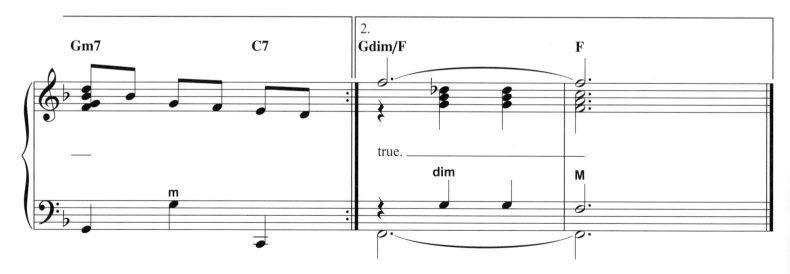

true.

THAT'S HOW YOU KNOW
from ENCHANTED

Music by ALAN MENKEN
Lyrics by STEPHEN SCHWARTZ

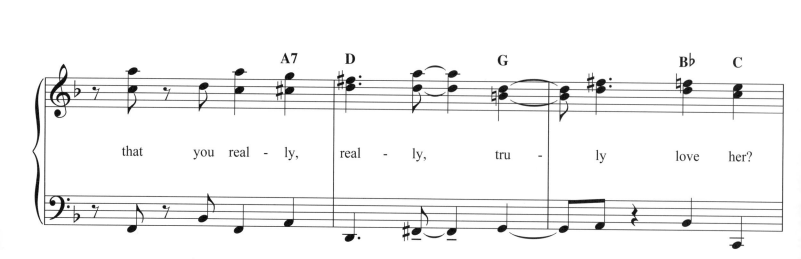

It's not e - nough to take ___ the one you love for grant - ed. ___

You must re - mind her, or ___ she'll be in - clined to

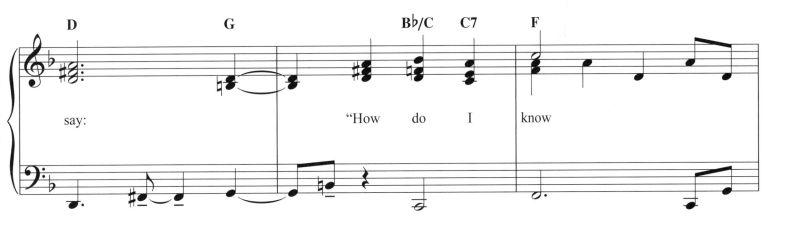

say: "How do I know

he loves me? ___ How do I

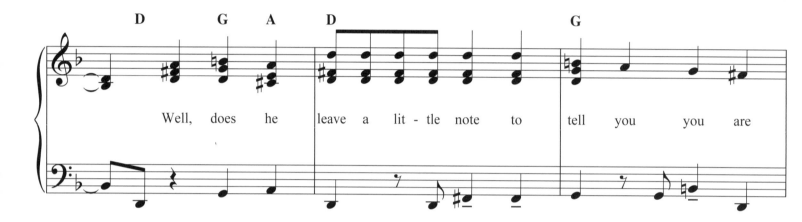

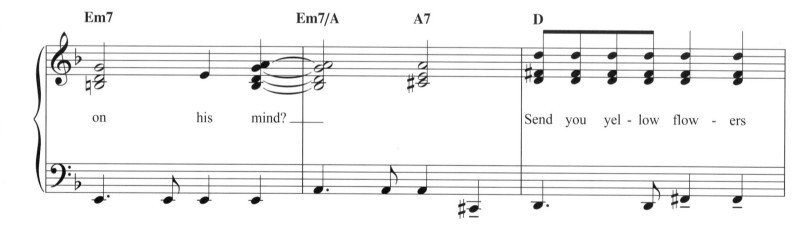

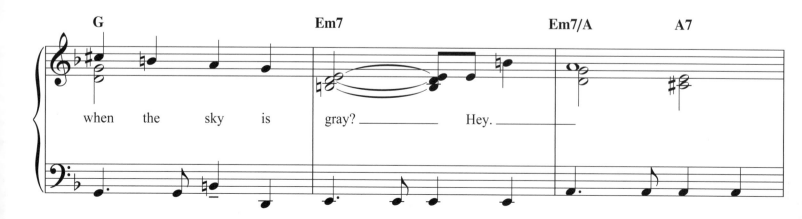

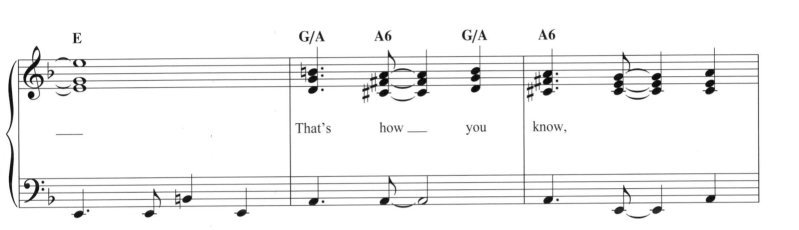

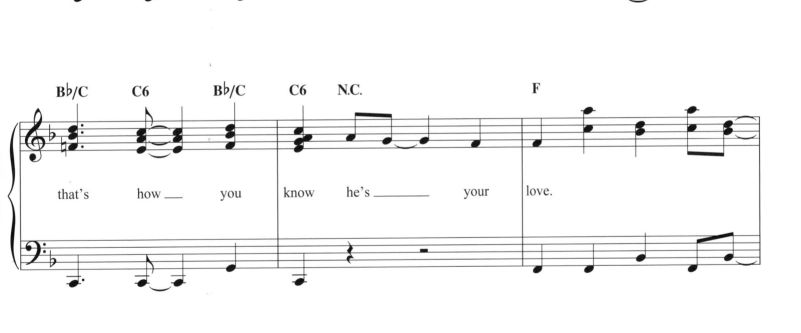

SPEECHLESS
from ALADDIN (2019)

Music by ALAN MENKEN
Lyrics by BENJ PASEK
and JUSTIN PAUL

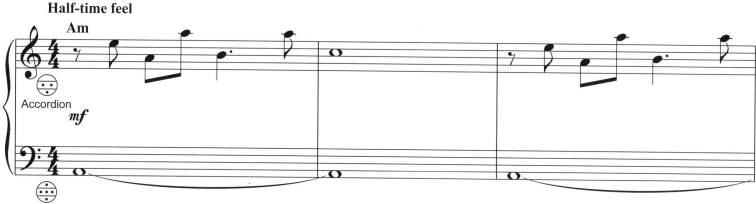

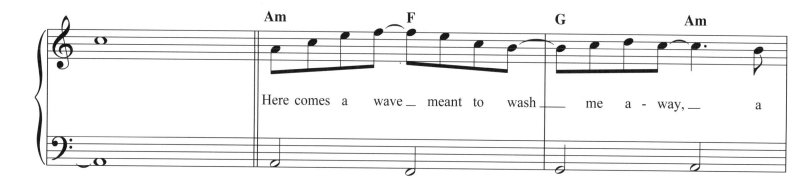

Here comes a wave ___ meant to wash ___ me a - way, ___ a

tide that is tak-ing me un - der. ___ Swal-low-ing sand, ___ left with noth-

- ing to say, ___ my voice drowned out ___ in the thun - der. ___

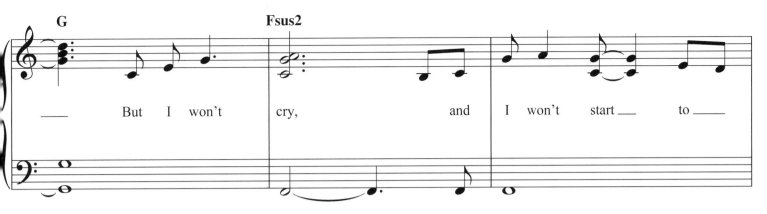

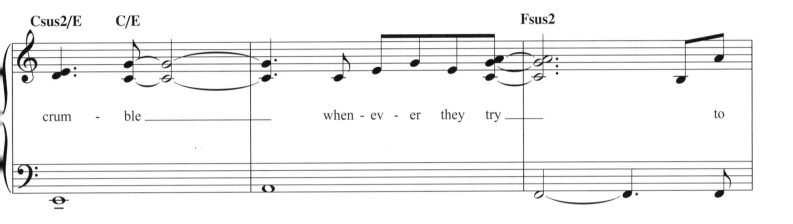

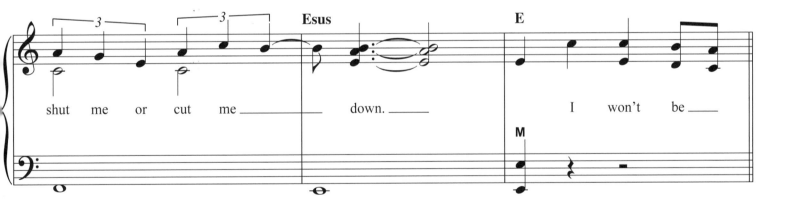

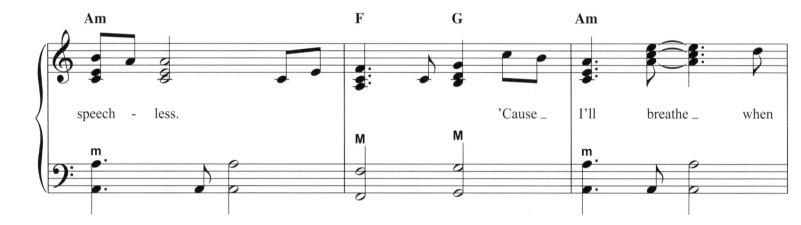

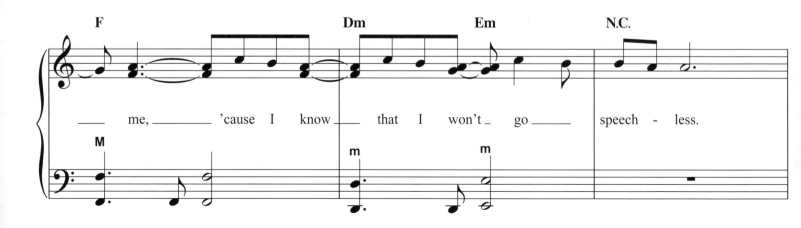

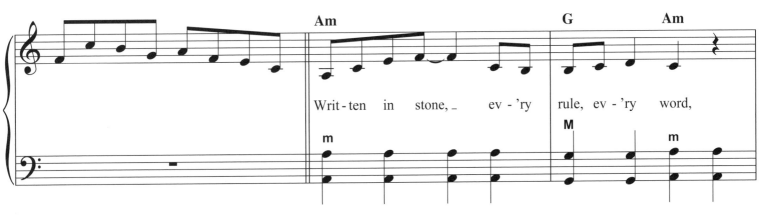

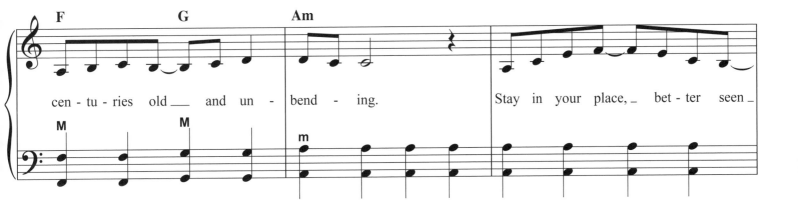

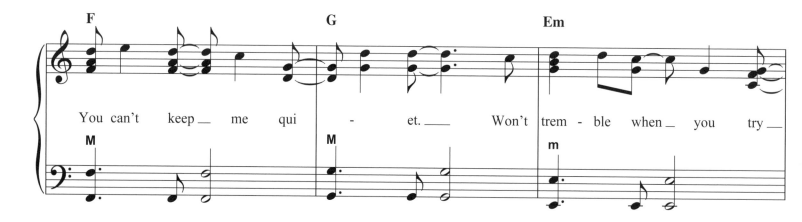

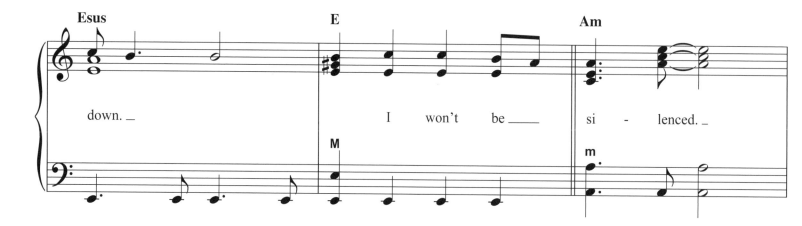

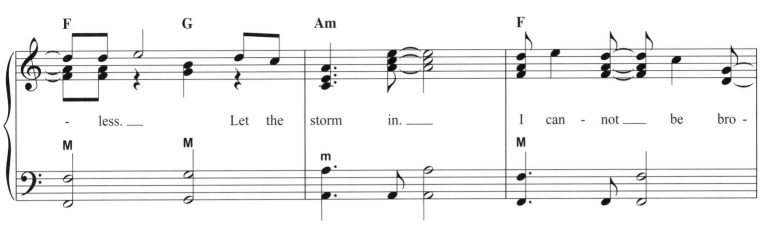

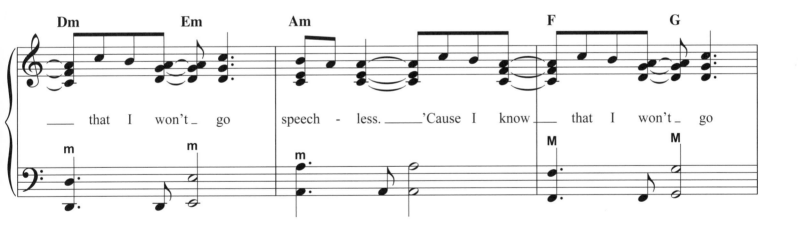

WHISTLE WHILE YOU WORK

from SNOW WHITE AND THE SEVEN DWARFS

Words by LARRY MOREY
Music by FRANK CHURCHILL

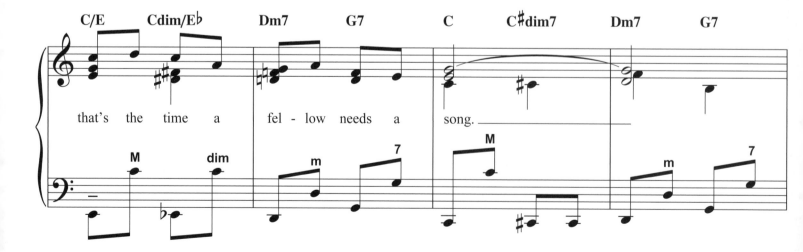

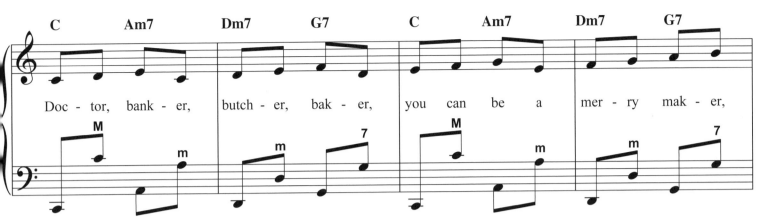

Doc - tor, bank - er, butch - er, bak - er, you can be a mer - ry mak - er,

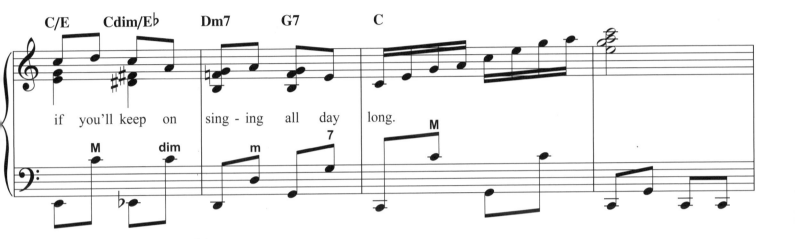

if you'll keep on sing - ing all day long.

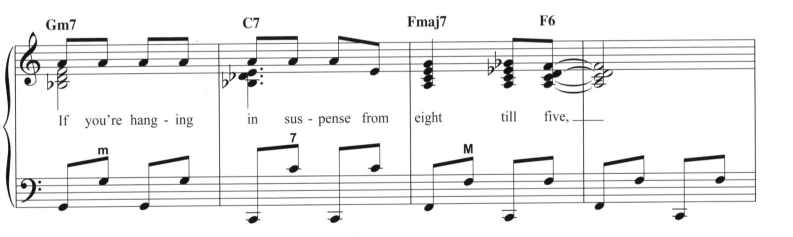

If you're hang - ing in sus - pense from eight till five, ___

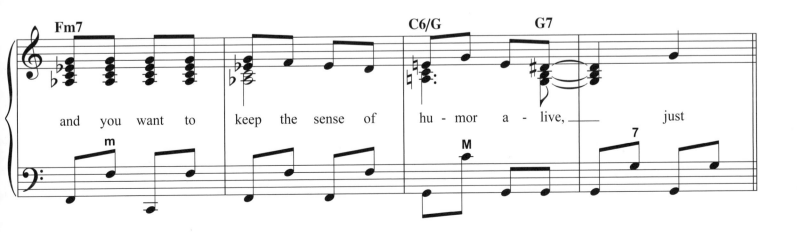

and you want to keep the sense of hu - mor a - live, ___ just

whis - tle while you work. Put

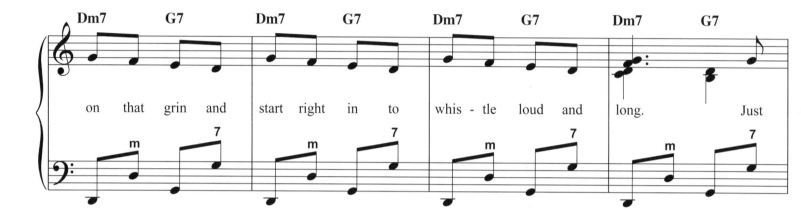

on that grin and start right in to whis - tle loud and long. Just

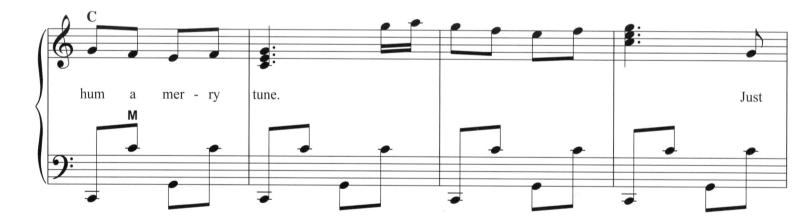

hum a mer - ry tune. Just

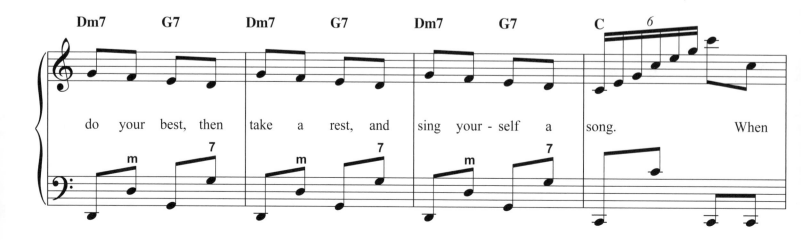

do your best, then take a rest, and sing your - self a song. When

there's too much to do, don't let it both - er you. For -

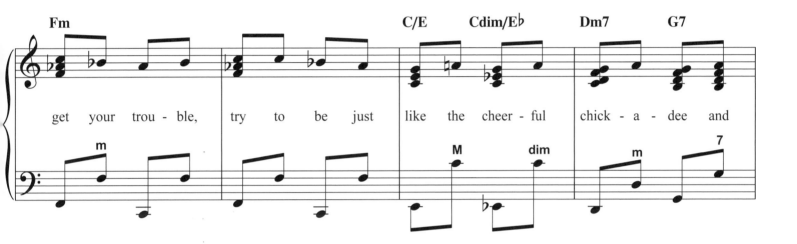

get your trou - ble, try to be just like the cheer - ful chick - a - dee and

whis - tle while you work. Come on, get smart, tune

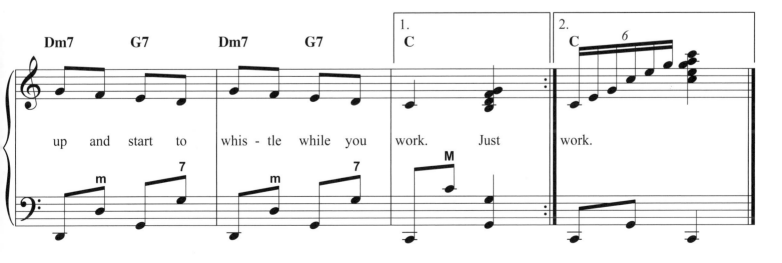

up and start to whis - tle while you work. Just work.

YOU'VE GOT A FRIEND IN ME
from TOY STORY

Music and Lyrics by
RANDY NEWMAN

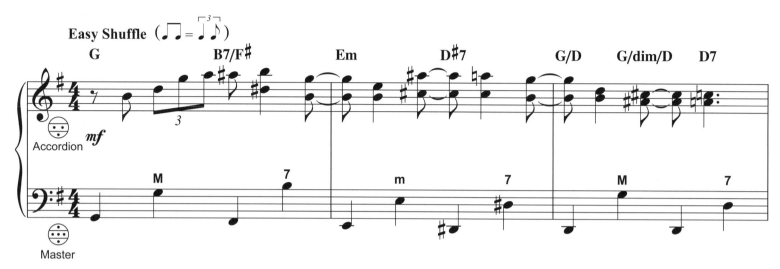

You've got a friend in me. ___
You've got a friend in me. ___

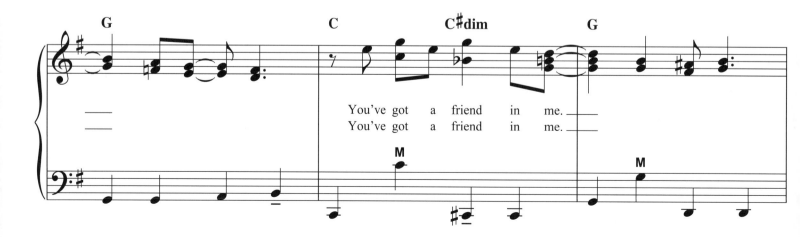

You've got a friend in me. ___
You've got a friend in me. ___

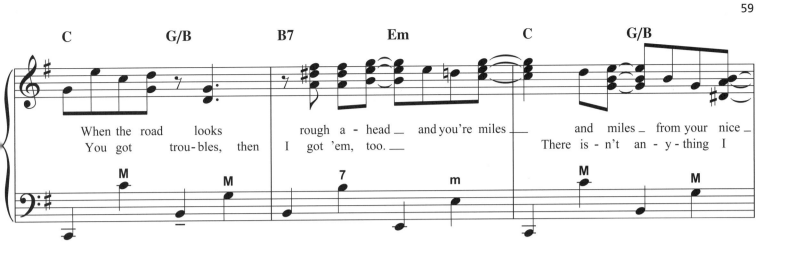

When the road looks rough a-head ___ and you're miles ___ and miles ___ from your nice ___
You got trou-bles, then I got 'em, too. ___ There is-n't an-y-thing I

___ warm bed, ___ you just re-mem-ber what your old pal said: ___ Son, you've ___
would-n't do ___ for you. If we stick to-geth-er we can see it through, ___ 'cause you've ___

___ got a friend in me. ___ Yeah, you've ___ got a friend in me. ___
___ got a friend in me. ___ Yeah, you've ___ got a friend in me. ___

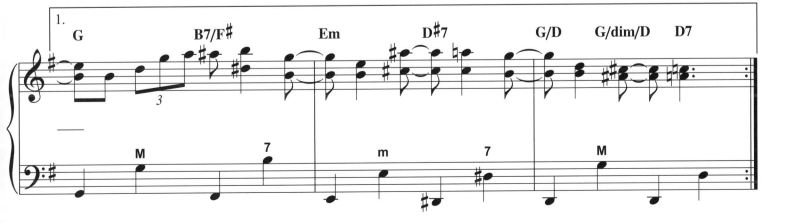

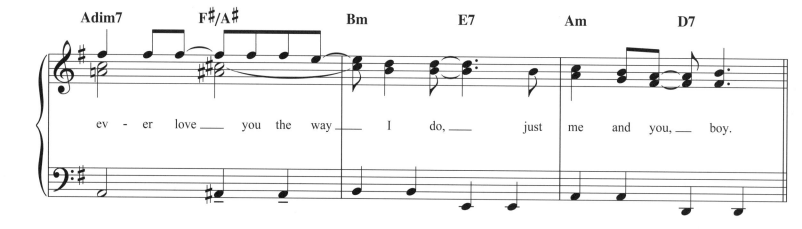

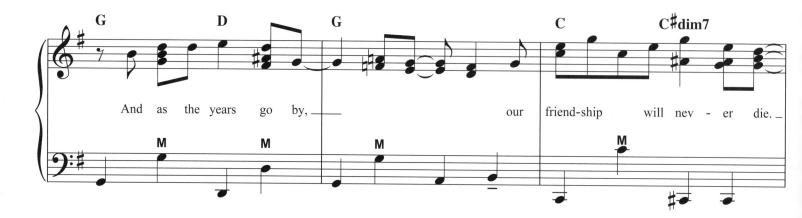

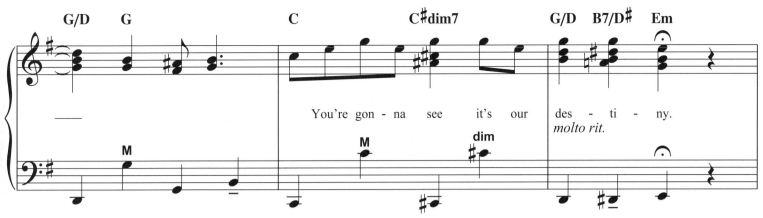

WHEN YOU WISH UPON A STAR
from PINOCCHIO

Words by NED WASHINGTON
Music by LEIGH HARLINE

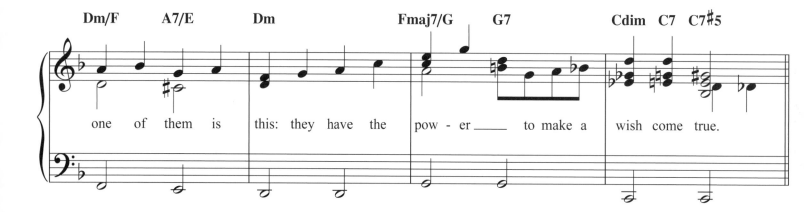

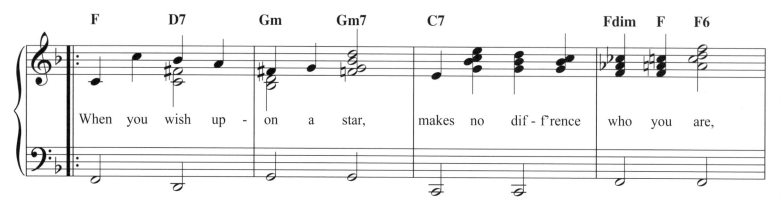

F/A   **A♭dim7**   **Gm7**   **C7**   **Fmaj7**   **Gm7**   **C7**

an - y - thing your heart de - sires will come to you.

F   **D7**   **Gm**   **Gm7**   **C7**   **Fdim**   **F**   **F6**

If your heart is in your dream, no re - quest is too ex - treme,

F/A   **A♭dim7**   **Gm7**   **C7**   **Fmaj7**

when you wish up - on a star as dream - ers do.

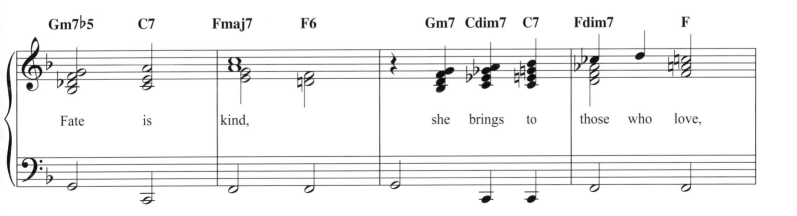

Gm7♭5   **C7**   **Fmaj7**   **F6**   **Gm7 Cdim7 C7**   **Fdim7**   **F**

Fate is kind, she brings to those who love,

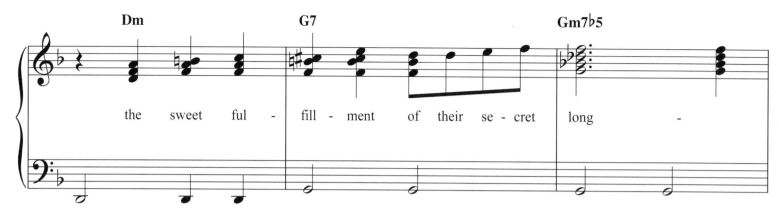

the sweet ful - fill - ment of their se - cret long -

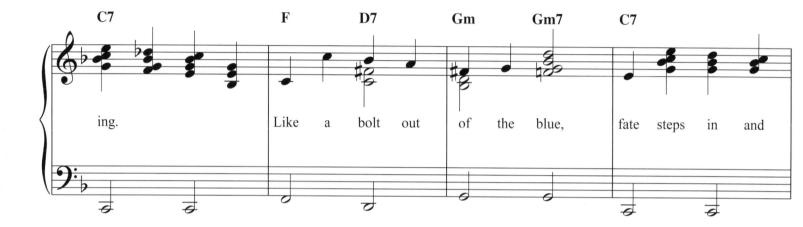

ing. Like a bolt out of the blue, fate steps in and

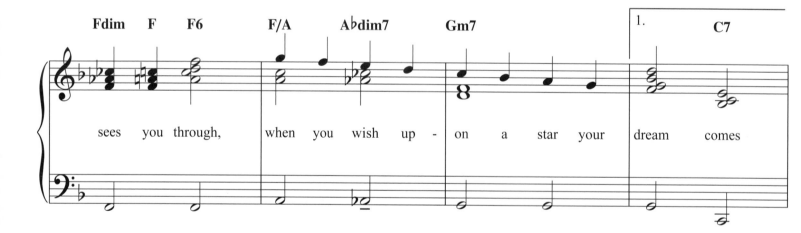

sees you through, when you wish up - on a star your dream comes

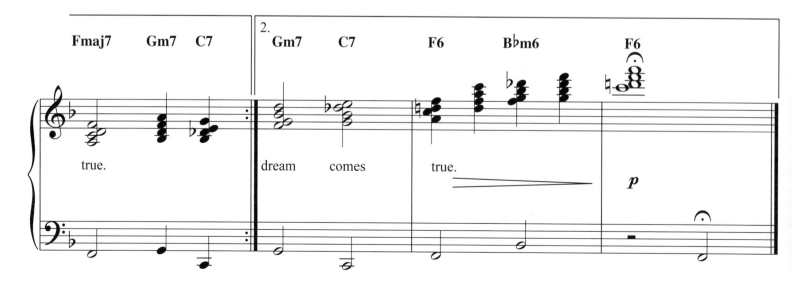

true. dream comes true.